Wings Without Birds

BRIAN HENRY is the author of five previous books—*Astronaut* (short-listed for the Forward Prize), *American Incident*, *Graft*, *Quarantine* (winner of the Alice Fay di Castagnola Award), and *The Stripping Point*. His work has been translated into Croatian, Polish, Russian, Serbian, and Slovenian. He has co-edited *Verse* since 1995. His translation of Tomaž Šalamun's *Woods and Chalices* appeared from Harcourt in 2008, and his translation of Aleš Šteger's *The Book of Things* is forthcoming from BOA Editions.

Also by Brian Henry

Wings Without Birds

Brian Henry

SALT

LONDON

PUBLISHED BY SALT PUBLISHING
Fourth Floor, 2 Tavistock Place, Bloomsbury, London WC1H 9RA United Kingdom

Salt Publishing 2010

Printed and bound in the United Kingdom by Lightning Source UK Ltd

Typeset in Swift 9.5 / 13

ISBN 978 1 84471 748 4 paperback

1 3 5 7 9 8 6 4 2

for Brynne, Tara, Beckett

Contents

Acknowledgements

Versions of most of these poems appeared in various print and online magazines between 1996 and 2009. Thanks to the editors of *Coconut, Conduit, Crowd, Elixir, Free Verse, Jacket, Lyric Poetry Review, Melancholia's Tremulous Dreadlocks, New American Writing, Overland, Poetry Ireland Review, Poetry Review, Puerto del Sol, Salt, Southwest Review, TriQuarterly, Volt, The Warwick Review,* and *Washington Square.* Special thanks to David Holler and Chad Sweeney at *Parthenon West Review* for devoting the space to "Where We Stand Now."

Epithalamium

What was I
but a cell in motion

the occasional collision

river   gutter   culvert

window through which I see you

the end-
point

near-mirage moored
at the horizon

to which the I in me
moved

as if there were still there

as if an I
is what I thought
                     to find there

     ~

And what was found there
when to you this I cleaved

(by I I mean a we)
(by we we mean a doubling
                                        —no thing halved)

When I say I
we are left to say it

When I see I
there are two there

Severance Pay

Let's say it was a splinter, for the sake of.
And this splinter was a metaphor for the wound-
inflicting data collecting behind your sinus
passages, waxing in pools every night before
sleep strikes its own pithy chords. *Thwip. Thwip*
thwip. And this splinter will not kill you
though its resilience raises the question
of how long you can last before you begin
to ease into what you call pain. The ceiling fan
at its lowest, the air barely moves through
the room, barely cuts the light from the street-
lamp as your daughter kicks you,
a heel against your kidney twice quickly,
before you can twist out of reach closer to the edge
of the bed you used to own. You find it easy to forget
and this blooms into its own source—of regret,
of sustenance—as, now, two and a half days later,
your daughter, that much older than when this began,
kisses you in her sleep on the back of the head.

To Toddle

The tension you carry inside you
—so fragile no image could usher—
produces what seems like a snapping
each hour, your body cycling

its fuel with such speed you are ever
sliding. Indentured to what
the body needs, you do not know
to pretend to be free from it.

Every action a link between "must"
and "must." Your days—they will move
without you. Will move you
unawares. Speak for you..

In the Neighborhood of Horses

Daughter who tells me the hills are a moon

and you're jumping over it
not two inches off the ground,

a baby tucked beneath an arm
as the other guides you both up

and then higher until you're
where you say it's warmth—

I'd like to sit and talk about
the right way to orchestrate

a network of needs and desires,
to distinguish one from the other

before the lies you're allowed are forbidden
and your flight never leaves

the ground so hot below you,
the moon you will soon outstrip.

Reign of Blisters

Swimming with Baby Alligator in the trench,
you hug it to you, stay afloat.
The rain unfurled by Hurricane Kate
seeps through the slab, the carpet drenched.
I uncoil the wet/dry vac in the garage,
the alligator wants to nurse—
it roots on your arm as it would the house,
does not know the house is a mirage
spun by weather patterns north of here.
Something is bound to drop soon.
That is the nature of atmosphere.
You yawn, acknowledge the moon
wiped clean by what dominates the near,
the sky, my sleep. This life, our cartoon.

I Wanted To Be Good

but the price was blue
and the house was wet

the couch cream
the dishes velvet

the desk was dying
a sweet summer death

the ankle was taped
the barre was hot

the mail was late
the walk was cracked

the meal complete
we wore earrings to bed

In the Neighborhood of Horses

To run in circles for no reason
is as noble an activity as any

as is to graze all day the grass
pulling itself through the clay

of the yard that slopes the rain
toward the house when it falls

carries the seeds you scattered
into the street marbled with tar

Abusing Another for the Sake of

Nothing gets in the way
of the fleas, they're starving
in the vacuum.
Who can blame them for leaping
all at once onto my babies
in the sunroom.
No eating kids
is what I hear lately. *No kicking.*
No biting. Daddy's vagina hurts,
Miss Donna eats dirt.
I like to touch the where
I bite, to see the pain
on the skin. It's why
my mouth returns again.
No blood yet.
Poor tongue,
you've managed so little
in the past four months.
I've touched you
to grass and sand
but prefer the gravel
that pools at the curb.
I eat the curb song,
can taste the riverbed
it came from, the tractor
that scooped it into a good.
O sun, muscle your way
past the dog's barking wall.
Yellow tractor, yellow sun, yellow dog.

In the Neighborhood of Horses

I have a piano,
it goes off and on.

Ladybugs in the hand vac,
stuck in the paint.

Paint in the hand vac.
Six shutters on the walk.

The sea is like an ocean.
That dog had its teeth prepared.

The hills roll the bad air in.

The Cassandra Complex

While water soaks through coffee grounds
and cereal grows soggy in the bowl,
the cricket under the sink discourses
on the dangers of original sin,
but our translator has the day off
and the advice goes unheeded. Besides,
you're busy writing your millennium
sequence, two thousand stanzas or so,
each line rhyming with Apocalypse.

Awake all night listening for the forecast,
I heard only static, the occasional trucker.
This kind of waiting is the hardest,
you say, your back nearly broken from the tedium.
Even the cat finds no solace under the sink,
the cricket's oratorical flare stunning it into delirium.
My arm burns from trying to turn forfeit
into profit. The cricket gathers his things
and leaves without a nod, without a word.

Housebound Mayhem,

                              there is a menace aswill
in the crawlspace, stripping the pipes of insulation.
The unsettled ghost of a previous inhabitant?
A raccoon burrowing, quick, from the cold?
Or just a figment, a fraction of you removed
and placed out of sight but not out of hearing?

Whatever, things still move on their own,
the house moans and wets itself, the walls
crack at the point they're expected to act
like ceilings, when all the walls want is to settle
for a century, welcome paint and paper alike,
and ignore every noise and its nuisant cause.

By Virtue of

The piano makes the same fucked-up noises
whichever corner we roll it into,
collects the same piles of books and paper.
The same dust.
                    What we need is a plan,
something to adhere to, like a rule, like
moisture, to avoid the pointless clutter.
Tidying the surfaces does not qualify
as a deep clean — mites still aggravate
sinuses, the stubs still gather
the stories of our days: how much light
and heat, where we were, were not, what food,
what broke, what we splurged on, could afford,
whom called, what vices, whom ignored.
Shredding them will erase us from us
— no journal to finger by, certainly no memory
— the songs we sang for each other:
though unpolished and unremembered,
the fact of them, the act and gesture of them,
are all that will remain after everything else
is swept up, removed and discarded, or stored.

The Term Loosely

Hairborne particles
brittle travelers

gawkward fandango
across the linoleum

vacuum the scalpage
littered like wrappers

chockfull of cabbage
or is it lettuce

ceramic scraped
to a scratchyard

moment swollen
with intent

backward formica
its wholesome sheen

every lick
to a shine

Bad Gardener

Butterfly bush
ravaged by inept hands
—inept hands with sheers—

so deformed
even the bees
stay clear

Irish Spring

Blind to the cat
that's never caught
a live thing

the hamster freaks
at the slightest
scent of seed

At the edge
of the yard
a deer sniffs

the soap hanging
to deter it
from the manicured

foliage

A Fine Piece of Equipment, Indeed

The clay works its slow way down the hill
to the concrete slab at the back door,
and this, since it has occurred all summer
through the drought, and because of the drought,
becomes an event, not unlike hating everyone
you know. You wonder if that's true or if you need
to cut back on the bourbon, get out more.
How misanthropic can you afford to be?
Quite.
      How does clay yawn? Rhetorically.
You don't wish physical harm on anyone,
you just want them to disappear
like the ants scuttling through.
               They drop
when they see you coming with the vacuum,
the carpet's casual threads providing cover
until you leave the room squinting and cursing
the intrusion of the natural world.
So many intrusions.
         You want to love,
to recall what that means, to stare
your way through a wall, the ceiling
until you are staring from what is called emotion
but the *but*'s and *though*'s and *yet*'s add up—
to nothing, of course, but also to something
like something. Why do you want to say "nothing
like something"? Because you evade
what you've set out to do, which is something
but, finally, nothing.
The vacuum's settings are locked in—
the switch has snapped and killed 4/5 of
your options—and the ants have noticed
but have not counted on you bending down

to pinch each between thumb and forefinger
until it pops, and though this is myrmicide
at its slowest, it's effective. Next in line: the spiders
in the corners, the roach in the kitchen cabinet.
The praying mantis on your arm, the walking stick
on your back. The termites you imagine
funneling the crawlspace like wanton similes,
rutting in the mulch pile at the top of the hill.

With Something Like Determination,
With Purpose

Incompetent retina, festooning the rainy lot.
The station has covering, you'll keep dry.

Rather than stand by the pump, please sit.
We're 600 miles from Falls Church, but why tempt?

I'm on my fourth espresso and it's still morning.
Immaculate turn. I am yawning.

I take rain personally, at least so early.
It keeps my head afog. I forget to umbrella

the pregnant, let them slouch through
the drizzle's lame attempts to saturate.

Decorating this cube could transform
the workspace into a place pleasant for work.

                    A throw rug, some paint.

A quarter-sized callous from the ball
of my foot the latest in the day's detritus.

Irresponsible of me, I know, to take
a death personally. Yet I feel lessened

by not having met him, Kenneth Koch,
and now I have his last book to get lost within.

May I say "And that is enough. More than
enough." If I did, would it be true?

How am I supposed to answer you, you ask,
and rightly so, for it is not my place to pose

questions, but to answer them. You're here
to see where I am leading you,

and though I was wanting to close the poem
with a mention of a poet I much admire

who recently passed, I am still moving,
working more from taste than from sight,

relying not at all on memory as I talk
my way through this part to Here.

It is cold out tonight, the first cold night
of the year. The garbage can, the recycling bins

wait at the driveway's mouth to be emptied
before dawn. The dogs next door barked

as I performed this weekly chore.
Now it is time for a glass of port.

Where We Stand Now

Because getting the mail means
crossing the street, the mailbox
in the neighbor's yard. The post
a white splinter. A monument
to your stepdad's MG and what
it can do after eight hours of—
Happy Hour from noon til.
You check the mail anyway,
that's what you do. Nothing.
No bills. Kids don't get those.
The thought itself signals you're years
past the event, which you conflate
with now, since you must cross the street
to check the mail, the mailbox beside
a telephone pole, almost
protected by it, and as long
as you've lived here, nothing
has happened to mailbox or mail.
This is where we stand now. Not
in our own yard. There, fire ants build
and move, swarm when I rake
them with a stick. One bit your friend.
I was out back moving mulch
that was a rotten stump, ground,
to the rear corner, to keep down
the weeds and vines, and heard him
scream his little-boy scream.
He cried for a while inside our house,
your mother iced his foot. I returned
to my shoveling a little undone.
Distinguishing one variety of plant
from another, even one unrelated,
has always been too much for me.
Poor vision, weak memory.
So when I pulled at the vines

ensnarling the fence, I did not know
I was making poison rain,
so much it soaked through cotton
to break out in streaks, shoulders to groin.
Like music, which I also forget / as soon
as silence. Proper names, place names.
Only numbers remain. Your daughter's
day in the center, the youngest but still.
She sings her own song, stretches up
to show how tall. Orders everyone
to eat once the talking is done.
Here, I think, this is a celebration
of the life that is you, that has become you.
This makes me happier than I have been
in months. And there is nothing external
about this. Despite the light rain
and its condemnation of sky.
The umbrella is uninvolved
but is being held to the side in case
its effect is required. I simultaneously
abhor and require. My focus, when it rains,
goes to my shoes, their ability
to withstand not just water but water
stains. And mud, the cold of the mud.
That day in Ljubljana was gray
but I could not smell rain when I left
the flat to walk the mile to town
and it hit not even halfway
there, so hard and fast it was
legendary rain, unreal
as my boots filled from below
and from above. They would not dry
and I had to buy shoes so ugly
you laughed when I brought them home
with their story, the boots left on a bench.

This is where we stand now. Behind the scene
where our daughter shines. She shines, so bright
I must look at you to make sure I am there,
that we have survived, made it this far
thus far. Once we start examining
lacks, we become what we loathe:
this is where we stand now, in a room
called an office in which no order.
Eighteen books on the desk, which shows
through as brown despite the papers
layering its veneer. Boxes on the floor.
A box in a chair. Trash can unemptied
for two weeks. Two stacks
of books in front of each case.
One empty chair. A phone, a stapler,
your coat hanging from the broken hook
on the back of the door. The sounds
of voices waffle through the tiles
of the ceiling, but the voices remain
in the room, beside or below you,
in which their owners speak. The volume
of the music here is increased, to drown.
Classical lines. I cannot remember who.
A cell phone's ring outside the office
crosses as if into, a young man speaks
loudly as if to you. You kick shut
the door, the umbrella falls from where
it was propped to block the way.
At fifteen I couldn't drink and walk,
I had to stop to sip. So many
who work in Athens' coffee shops
have tattoos just above the ass.
Their work requires them to turn
their backs on customers and bend,
which raises their tops and bares the ink.

What at first allured is now tired.
Now plain skin would arouse.
You are not prepared to confess now.
To pick up an idea is an idea.
To dodge an idea is another.
The library's steps should be free
of smoke. The library's steps
should be for stepping. The library's
columns hold up the fountain
of knowledge. Bless them.
Will the refusal of tweed purify me?
Keep me pure? At fifteen I wanted
elbow patches. I owned
a blazer at fifteen. Is it too late
to atone? I bought a pair of boots
I never wore after Whelan asked
if they were from the girls' department.
I'd thought they were sleek.
This is where we stand now. On a sidewalk
before the crosswalk waiting for the red
to turn to white, for word to become image.
Out and out, we push ourselves,
only to return as quickly as possible
to where we felt the push to leave.
You pick up a sonnet and test it,
you dodge a sonnet and divest yourself
of distillation. Is common knowledge
borrowed knowledge? Would you say
it's citeable? Does that make you
richer? enriched? Let's not talk
ill of the dead. Just the dying.
You wonder if my problem is listening
or remembering. If both, then it's caring.
What do you want for your birthday?
To forget. I want a ribbon

so I can connect this spool to that
and type letters to the editor.
My leg dangles numb from my knee.
The body, my body, is what
I think about most. Even in my sleep
I think about thebodymybody.
How it disappoints in every way.
I consider hiring another
to replace this body but. Without
which aside from on top of
entranced by outward switch
a stretch to teach the body how
to stretch *and* strengthen. The tops of my feet
—pathetic little bones—hurt.
I snipped a peeling blister from one
and forgot to wash. What did I forget
to wash and for how long forgotten?
Caffeine is no substitute for sleep
though sometimes it breathes like a meteor
shower that peaks an hour before dawn.
You woke for it but the moon was full
and, your glasses downstairs in the cold,
you thought you saw clouds. Muldoon
in the paper, not even a week after
his visit. Proper names: Heaney,
Donne, Korelitz, McGuckian,
Carson, Davison. There are others
but they have been forgotten. Call them
e, f, g. Call them a triangle
and thank them for connecting. Open forms
close down. Next to the poet
a Victoria's Secret ad with a woman
—hair blond and long, legs long—
in a black sheer something in front of
a mirror. The curves of her ass,

with its crack, the cleft where it meets
her legs, highlight the material's benefits,
but the image has been altered: a blank
space has replaced what should be hair
given the fabric and its sheerness.
The look on her face defies complaint,
but you complain anyway, do not buy
the product. The poet sits on steps,
unaware of his partner on the page.
I listen for the sound of skin about to rip
but hear only a flutter as if the wind
were urging itself to involve.
Not a defense mechanism, this
movement between "you" and "I,"
but a deflective mechanism meant
to hold and to resist the self and its secrets.
You refuse to read poems as pixels,
I defuse the difference and call it
visual criticism. You decline
to laugh and I decide you are right
in your decline. I hold
this ancient vase, this artifact,
and place it in front of me and sit down
to write a poem—I have a meter,
a rhyme scheme, a first line ("The curves
in clay enhance this paltry past"),
the meaning of ekphrasis in me;
"last" will rhyme with "past," the poem
will go to fourteen lines—and I realize
I know nothing about the vase,
its past or place, the way it took to here,
and feel almost afraid, or sick,
on its behalf. I write the poem
anyway. How it shines.
A missed appointment—not mine—

and me sick. Made to feel. Sick.
Unstarched and frigid on a day colder
than expected. Thus the forecast.
Heidi and John plan to start something,
need a name. *Wagon. Trestle.*
Scarf. Red umbrella. A word
neither pretentious nor taken.
A word, perhaps, that sticks
to this place without the provincial,
the cute, or the stupid. A missed
appointment and I am bad. Stupid.
Not a walking calendar.
Not a sorry mess. My point
of reference lost, I waylay
a flier posted at the coffee shop.
Vaginal yet phallic, like a slip-
per. Boredom a possibility,
never an option. Enhance the learning
experience by improving
the learning environment.
Wrap autumn around you
and come like it counts for once.
Resist winter and what withers with it.
Decline to weep for what is no longer
a what but a was. This chain of what was:
these mistakes allowed twice.
Once in their occurrence, twice
in their recalling. The country prepares
to attack, the country assumes.
Is smoking pot with Powell's
daughter news? Newsworthy?
Is her lover's loving others in his loft,
emerging between to borrow (read:
take) a rubber? And how long ago
was that? Just after the first Gulf War,

just before Clinton popped in.
The sign of a poem's greatness is not
if I want to sit down and memorize it,
but if I want to kill who wrote it
so I can claim it. I am dying
just like everyone else
is dying: daily. Barely
into this poem and the daily
keeps seeping in. Politics
etcetera. And I began
from love and wanting to write from love.
The need for anger has a way.
To read the news is to see, to see,
to see. To hear the news is to read,
to read. Undead, I die slowly,
watch the hair flee my scalp
at every opportunity,
watch the skin lose. One benefit
of myopia is not being bothered
by such things too much, as I see
little once I walk in and de-lens.
Cleaning a low priority,
there is no dirt to clean. This house
is trying to kill me with its dust
and bad air. Too much drift
everywhere. No room is safe
from the ground, the stale sounds.
The Royal smashed beyond fixing
during the move, I set to it
with a screwdriver to remove as much
of it from itself as I can. Arrive.
I arrange the screws to spell "pain"
and photograph the word with the type-
writer's husk surrounded
by pieces of its former self then

throw it all into a box and drive
to the Clarke County landfill.
The car has new tires, new belt,
its floor covered with raisins
Cheerios barrettes pretzels
paper and if I were a crying man
I would cry I swear I would.
Luna's *Live* does not improve me
despite the wish. If I chose *Sea Change*
or anything by Nick Drake,
would I kill myself finally or simply
wish I could afford the wine I've stopped
drinking because I cannot afford.
Crack this poem open and you will see
me seated with headphones on, glasses
off, a shirt I bought thirteen years
ago, pants not so old but button-
less, socks the newest thing
on me, my body losing
its occasional fleshiness
growing lean because I dis-
trust food and what it does
because I am learning to move
and cause pain by moving because
I am sitting here wanting to keep
going, to reach, knowing I will keep
going. Has there been a you today?
How many have dropped into
the poem today? My one chance
is to surround myself with those
I love, and what began with love
today began with an appointment
(not mine) I missed, and this has led
to what I would prefer to leave
behind. Tomorrow I will leave it

there unless the air remains
remains. The air so unclear here,
I finger my eye trying to coax a—
Handle the garbage to the curb,
separate the recyclables,
break down a large box
to lay flat and see gone.
I will not push a fist through glass
tonight. Forgive me, me, but I must
resist a scar that easy to read.
All reading is mis-reading.
The angle of approach is only part
of it. The glass will eat the skin
without focus the skin will inhale
the glass without speed and focus
there is no snap at the end to carry
the skin into and out of the glass
before the meat of the hand the knuckles
the wrist are cut so clean you feel
the air as pain. Air descends
to announce the violation of skin.
Who needs a lungfull of that in a limb?
This is where we stand now. On the verge
of acting in our own worst interests.
Sorry to have missed the point.
(Two days off and everything
is off. Today I drove to the edge
of Georgia. Lake Hartwell's red shore
from a bridge. Now I'm a Southern poet!
The sun in my rearview so loud
I had to hold up a hand.
It set hard, and the moon—moon
shadow you're "hipping and hopping" on.
Until beset upon by clouds.
No more moon. The further north

I drove the more southern I felt.
No, not Southern. Georgian.
Georgia poet! Driving with *Merriment*,
Up, Left To His Own Devices,
Reveal, and for the last hundred miles,
In the Aeroplane Over the Sea.
People say Athens does not count
as the South. I count myself out.)
Pre-Thanksgiving and already
we give our thanks. Every time
I look your way I give thanks.
The unelected president
decides to burn a DVD
and shoves the disc into the toaster.
The ad is banned, poor England.
Your humour sacked by the war on terror!
Fuckwits yawn over their very old
wines and poke holes. So many
the light cannot find a way through.
If I wrote religious tracts,
the meter would not jitter
as it moves. Four punches per line
does not always equal four
feet though it could, it could.
An East Brunswick afternoon,
leftover noodles and veggies,
we drove to, were talking about.
Belfast, of course, is no Dublin.
Now let's talk about me
for a change. The holly by the window
blocks your view of the oak beyond it,
freakish in how it grows despite
the brown air and brown water
that feed it. Please do not eat the snow,
no matter how white. Bones are not

to be taken for granted; remove one
and see what I mean. What I mean
is every part of me is a part
of something and should remain
a part of something. To forget
and let a part of something slip.
What if the part you lose is what
makes you sensitive to others'
suffering? This is where we
stand now. Between the lines
yet straight, in need of sexuality
whatever its bent. Reason
enough to lay off and let people come
where they want to come. I know
I've said nothing profound yet,
so clearly something else is at work.
A different agenda. An attempt
to hold my thoughts all at once
in a single column and maintain
the look and feel of order however
order arranges itself. Distance
less essential to this than to what
was written before. An attempt
at stepping to the side of anger and what-
ever else moved me to write
before. And I know the meta
holds less interest now than. To make
poetry a fiction. Dissolved
the speck of paper on my tongue
and called what I saw a vision.
Nourished by the lackadaisical
for too long, I converted to high-
strung. Too ashamed to answer "me"
when the father of my daughter's friend
asked (rhet.) "Who wants to be

an orthodontist when they grow up?"
I felt a little better when he turned
the talk to how much they make.
I just thought it would be nice to force
wayward teeth to grow straight.
Five in the kitchen, doors open
for the smoke. The neck is burning.
I have not seen the gizzard. I ate one
once. You asleep in your party dress
behind me on the bed, Luna still
in the laptop. You awoke at six,
cried when we told you to hush,
screamed until I wanted to punch
myself in the mouth to make you stop.
Baby E is asleep, you'll wake
the baby you'll wake the baby you'll.
If you could write off the time I donate
to charity, would you donate my time
to charity? Could a poem
be called a charity? A child?
Something there does not equate.
This is where we stand now. On both sides
of a common bed. Your birthday almost
two weeks old and the presents still
trickle in. If I call this poem a journal
does that settle anything? make
anything less or more clear?
If I choose blueberry cream cheese
over strawberry, does that amount
to treason? How many murders
in the name of some god? If I misspell
Mahommed, who will issue the fatwa?
You can have my head, Allah. My spine.
You can bend me over, Christ. I stand
here waiting to be ravaged by belief

I myself do not hold. I believe in what
I see and then don't always believe.
The Fates are as likely a source of life
as any god with balls and a prick.
If I insist on doubt, who will set me
on the path to faith if not the god(s)
I've pissed off with doubt? This gets old,
I agree. I agree that "veer" should be applied
only to birds under attack
by other birds. Three days later
a finch shits on Megan's poem.
She tries not to take it personally.
Donn asks what the white is
in chicken shit, and I answer piss.
Chicken shit, he says. Ah,
a joke not a question. Duh.
I will myself beyond the body
in front of me, and my foot goes.
Pat me on the head and call me drizzle.
The convection heater helps,
the foam on the inside of the frames.
However you pronounce it, nu-
clear war is not a round of golf
or a coke binge. Let go of your cock
long enough, fella, and you might
learn something. Like people do not
have to die by the thousand for you
to keep your retirement plan.
Why isn't there a video game
where one can assassinate
the fucker? We all live in the mind.
This is not a recording, nor
is it real. Tuck the hamster is typing
this; he is a far cry from Nip
his predecessor, who won the battle

and lost the war. I need a pet
to shave my beard and trim the hair
that sprouts from my ears. To rub my ass
and pry the dirt that sticks at the back
of my navel. Rock and roll fucks
with every theory of the avant-garde.
Can the avant-garde advance
on a G4 PowerBook?
It will play a DVD
it will burn a CD and strip
the sheen of difficulty from every
endeavor. It pumps Cobain's
anger and pain into both ears
and pushes Tuck off the keyboard
so a man can step up and weep
for what was/what is/what will, now,
never be. Binge, binge, purge.
It's the Friday after Jesus'
day and I'm in New York
which makes this a New York poem.
Yes, it really is that simple.
I'm allergic to newspaper,
to money when it's new. I'm afraid
of coins and the grime they leave.
Everyone speaks in code.
I hate parties so I go to the party,
finally meet J., who saves
the encounter with a joke I like.
M.'s been drinking all day,
Joe tells Jen that art cannot "convey"
a spanking. Jen, an artist, will not
agree. The issue is less art
than spanking. It's all about spanking.
This is where we stand now. On the brink
of expatriation. Brought

to a drool, Americans out-
spent themselves this Christmas.
Caught by accident in a crowd,
I am not free from the lines
for the rink the tree Radio City
Music Hall for half an hour.
Timothy has gone to see friends
but Lynn is home to let me
and my luggage in. We meet Brett
for coffee at The Fall. A hooker
on the subway slides over
to make room for me. I force
myself not to touch my wallet
to be sure it's there and hate
myself for thinking about it
at all, here, and now. Which is where
we stand now. On the edge of a new year
that, so far, is a bad year.
Ignore what is here and consider
the dinosaurs, how much is known now
compared to when you last cared.
Let me be the first to say: this mess
is far from perfect, or "perfect," which
is not where we are standing now but where
we just were standing, toward the back
of the crowd chatting, knowing the three
on the stage were uptight about noise
from the crowd, "SHUT THE FUCK UP"
filtering from the center of the floor
lest Yo La Tengo despise our town
for good. When they replayed a song
—"I don't think you heard [read:
appreciated] that one"—we left.
A club is not a congregation,
a group cannot assume silence

without earning it or making it
moot through music. Beyond
the woodpile between our yard and theirs,
the dead tree creaks and rocks
with the wind until its limits
force it to stop and it stops
and returns to its initial position
but then moves past it again
and though leaning into the wind
the tree pushes into it until
the wind pushes it back on its own
rocking, not a procedure
but a process dependent on several
things for its significance: the tree,
the wind, the yards, and me. It falls
and flattens the grass below. So much
penetralia with which to contend.
So many flavors. Dust mites
die when the heating system scalds
the interior. At the allergist's
I reacted to every prick of the skin.
This is where we stand now. In a welt
on the arm that burns it itches so hot.
A piñata spilled, pick out
the choicest pieces and chew, as on
a series of fragments arranged alpha-
betically. I crank the a/c
despite the bill. Close the blinds
to spite the sun. Clog the drain
to spite the drain. Unsung where-
ever drywall reflects a house's
attempts to settle back down,
this is where we stand. Now,
with twenty-four minutes to write
the next, the battery slowing

to nil. So drunk I lost sight
of what I was seeing, a shift
from vertical to less than straight,
the daily task presses what's left
of my brain after it sheds its weight
gathered from a day of so much speech
the lips have chapped. Today no one
wept though pollen seemed to reach
inside the building—sniffly afternoon.
With sixteen minutes, and only two lines,
I realize I do not realize.

19 Nov–29 Dec 2002, 13 March 2003, 8–14 May 2003

Impossible Hypotenuse

Now that RPMs are irrelevant
I consider music a lost
case in point. I refuse to listen.
A state of emergency is broadcast,
the garbage disposal doesn't grind,
it hums. Leaky pipe leaky joint.
If I don't allow myself corny jokes,
clunky puns, then how far from
Point A can that Publix balloon,
now a freckle on the sky,
get before its helium is forced
by the atmosphere to lurch through
the latex and send the scrap
with its ribbony string back down?
If we drive fast and with purpose,
we can measure AC, but not BC,
and therefore not AB, so when
my daughter, who let the thing go
as I fastened her into the car,
asks where her balloon went,
I let myself wish I believed
or that balloons had spirits
that rise when their earthly flesh
is spent. But I do what all good
atheist parents do: tell her to ask
her mother then change the subject,
relieved I don't believe.
That might sound like an epiphany
or like I'm offering some closure,
a moment where, when I read this
to you, you can feel justified
in chuckling or groaning one of those
groans that poisons so many publics.
I'm not here for epiphanies,
I don't want to hear you

groan. What makes me sad
about the dead (John Forbes, say):
the dead don't read poems,
and if they did, they would think
it's all crap. And it is, John, it is.

Wings Without Birds

I'll see you soon, Tomaž,
but want to prepare
the ground for your coming,
you for your arrival.
                Sky clear,
slight wind, temperature
two months ahead of schedule,
my back hurts less than usual.
Herniated disk, early arthritis.
You hurt, too: why I mention this.
Overnight a rare thunderstorm
left a mist to peer through.
Lightning never less than
two miles away, its partner
once rolled for half a minute.
Tara, sleep-nursing, said
she and her brother thought
thunder was the sound of God
bowling. Lightning, a strike.
Despite the mix-up of cause-
effect, the image has legs.
So perfect, He nails
a strike before the release.
And what would Zeus think?
Pegasus' wings singed,
Geryon blasted to a shrivel.
The mist will lift, I promise.
The mailman will ensure
the day you arrive is blessed.
God, he says, will take care
of my back. (And yours?)
And Zeus? He's still pissed,
wanting to fuck but stuck in the past.
He never did adapt. There is no
"standing room for his progeny."

Yet we still have the ostrich,
the condor.
                    A bald eagle nests
near our house for the winter.
It will leave before you're here,
taking with it its knowledge
of what happens "when the stamens
of a flower suddenly spring
towards the pistil, or slowly move
one after the other towards it."
Some days it circles above
the street, we never see it land.
Two nights ago I dreamed
of snakes in the mulch out back,
trying to split them with a stick,
to decide which to kill first.
One burst, the other got away.
A brown recluse lives in the compost,
a black widow under a garden stone.
A copperhead asleep under the leaves
woke when I raked it. Of course I killed it.
Only God can strike before striking,
everyone else must test her luck.
We live at the entangled bank.
Your back, I know, can floor you.
Take your pick when you're here.
Heating pad, heated seats. Port
and ibuprofen, beer and aspirin.
We even have an iron, should your spine
require its adjustible touch.
A rocket still hangs in the oak
just above the squirrels' mass of leaves.
If it falls between now and you,
it's yours.
                    The unsplit wood

(diseased tree) flanks the compost heap.
When you come, clover will cover
the center of what was a garden.
The sun will glance off and augment
the green among the surrounding brown.
The bank beams.
                    Rain now against
the storm window, the deck sags.
A hole has opened up beneath.
Beside the butterfly bush, a jangle
of thorns. The roses might show.
I want to rise with you above the view
given by the kitchen window,
hover to watch the earth's teeming,
the gutters and roof soggy and worn.
Hammocked beside you in the breeze-
less tree, I'll close my weaker eye
and will away our pain: it will seep up,
above, not into, the tree.
When we descend, be sure to land
where the ground is soft—well away
from slate and stones and thorns
and rotting deck.
                    The bank will receive us,
fold us into the mix. We will remake
the garden, expel every god and beast.

Where Hannibal Whomped the Romans

1.

The wood chips beneath the swingset
meant to shield the trapeze fall,
halt that broken collar bone, wretched neck,
thwart the tears and globs of snot,
and make the arena safe for stunts,
home now to garden spiders and fire ants,
a catching ground for weaker leaves
and grey squirrels' unwanted nuts,
this spread and locus, contained by mulch
and timbers, rebar no grass can touch—

2.

The giant blue ball curves as it descends,
is slick and hard to catch.
Its purple counterpart nuzzles a shrub
and leaks, will be flat in a week.
The third ball, smaller and harder,
considers itself a weapon:
stiff projectile to bloody a nose,
knock the wind out of, bruise a limb.
On occasion one is lifted by the wind,
moved elsewhere in the yard.

3.

The dragonfly wing held to the windshield
       by the wind
unsticks when lifted at a stop.
       Under the lens
the lines scatter into a city grid
       before buildings
intrude on the intersections and angles.
       A constellation
of potential, nothing actual or acted upon:
       a clean sheet.

4.

The hidden shoes—payback for the one
who excludes—call forth the confrontation
by the slide, where three corner one
and demand, press and demand.
The scene ends without blood or bruise.

Later, the cornered cracks open
the purse of the personal to divulge
the backstory, what was on her mind:
which of the three to kick first, where,
and how hard. She held off that urge.

5.

The dread of routine and the comfort,
the alarm and the tucking-in:
a balance beam of serpentine design.

We weave along unafraid to fall
and fearing the twisted ankle or scrape,
the shock of the sudden horizontal.

We refuse the elevator, its closing-in,
and launch our bodies up the stairs,
ignoring the gaps between each step,
hands sliding up the rail, a rough skim.

6.

Black widow beneath
        an upturned rock,
        —undarkened spot—
split by the trowel,

your black widow partner-
        neighbor also under,
        flipped, crushed
by a smaller stone:

you put my shine to shame,
        put me to shame.

Crawlspace

The wind crosses
through the vents

stirs the spores
and cellulose debris

the rotting wood
the mites beneath

and then swoops
flees the house

and what's below
for the sun

knowing the sun
will level it

with its flame
of zero gaze

that bastard sun

Neither Did the Trees nor Stones Remain
Any Longer in Their Places

The oak would hold the girl as far as the roofline
but above the roof it tapered to a thinness
unfit for human weight.
                              The girl knew this,
told herself this even as she climbed.

The first branch to bend almost to breaking
within arm's reach of another branch,
the girl held onto both—
                              the first branch
returned, remained in the girl's hands, shaking.

A branch for each hand and for each foot,
the girl lifted herself at last above the house,
and from that height she saw a second house—
the abandoned one in the neighboring lot.

That house had burned last year.
                              A winter fire.
But there it stood, untouched by flame, prepared
for some family to move in.
                              Unsure where
to place herself, the girl, though sore and tired,

held to that tree until there was no sun
to guide her (safely) back down.

What To Do With a Fat Rope of Old Vine

This panorama extends to subtler regions
where a stone remains a stone
and the field somehow becomes a thing to lean on
despite the malfunction of vision
as soon as the sun withdraws.

As soon as the girl withdraws
the field becomes a thing to rein in
despite the function of vision
where "stone" ruins a stone.

A stone recalls a stone
despite the infraction of vision
as soon as the girl exhales
the field, a subtle thing to withdraw.

Somehow the field withdraws
the girl despite the failure of function.

As soon as a stone returns to a thing
the girl returns to her vision.

Life's Better on the Porch

To visit, from the street,
a house you lived in as a child
is to strain to see the tops
of trees you could once vault with ease
before someone put up a fence,
the basketball goal, the ornamental
wheelbarrow on the once-white porch,
the railing of which you leapt
to chase down and pummel a friend
who ignored your command to keep off
the seedlings that, with water and time,
would establish this now-hardy yard,
which was struggling to catch
when the kid tried to undo what nature
would have done but was doing too slowly:
shape a half-acre into something
like a home, or what one driving by
would think to call a home
regardless of the air within,
on the other side of the still-black steel door,
which never stuck when it rained.

Materniliad

Your polite skin stretches aisle-
ward, immediate horizon,
would turn if there were
a bearing.
         The machines work
through the night, cleaning
the air and watering the air.
The glass of ice holds its straw,
the pills in place beside the glass.
Winter digested, the furnace
will not click on, suck moisture.
"The prison of your tongue
within the prison of your sleep
watered me with a beautiful
easy . . ." a sleeptalking thought.
The house splits as it settles,
the carpet shrinks toward
the center. The yard shrinks
toward the center.
              —A wasp
in the house clunking against
the walls until it, too, shrinks
toward the center. That is where
the broom finds it. The bristles.
Its torn body dragged through
the streets of the house then back
to the center. Nothing of substance
remains.

Family, Portrait

And your hand in my lap
as if unleafed beneath
the fibers of the untent
so soaked
the condensation is more drip
than incipient wet.
I nudge your hand away,
the better to govern
the bites slathered in hydrocortisone.

And me scratching well before dawn
until dawn the two on my calf,
the moisture on the roof
showed itself, a minor threat.
If only I could slip out
of my body, or assault skin
with such focus a layer or two
falls to reveal a purer me.
The shovel I used for the trench
along the back of our house
took my right palm,
part of my left.
I could not lift or hold anything
without pain.

Now, upon waking, you
are offered some
of our daughter's energy.
She whooshes it onto you
but your brain will not move
with the new day
even as the day pokes forward
and morning is pushed
away with the moisture.

I am coughing the chlorine
the bourbon did not neutralize.
Caffeine the shadow spouse,
it cunts the sun;
your head will explode without it,
you say, the energy still there
outside you.
Drinking until the birds
announce the change in light.

Our June song makes peace
with lack of sleep, enforces
idleness. Bites, burns, the film
of the outdoors that covers us,
family, as soon as we rise
unshowered and uninterested,
unready for everything around us.

This Route
Plymouth-Wentworth, NH

Perfidy on the outskirts, this casual sniping
little more than
$\qquad$ breakfast at noon,
breakfast at midnight, breakfast
of what one released. In between,
cheese. Forks can't lift it,
the wickedness.
$\qquad$ The diner's bulge—
vinyl growth on its '50s metal core—
signals new owner.

That funeral procession last November
reminded the remaining to cherish
their waistlines while they're there.
Carbs, fats, saturated fats, vitamin D.
Proportion, not portions, the issue
of the hour.
$\qquad$ That and the passion.

The heron rejects the river,
we reject the heron, fish
bottles out, test each rock
with our asses, motorcyclical
in design, and placate our craving
for landscape for the next 12 miles
where every spot is out-
skirt, before everything just stops—

an exercise in something.
Ruins? Perspective? Oxidation?
Enriched by what remote
has brought us, we beckon,
begging to be enhanced.

All that we see gives in. We, grown.
Oxygen entranced, a different pollen.
Every thing is more open out here.

❖

Sometimes

swift, sometimes
sparrow
           or gray squirrel

sprawled between trees

or no bird
but a whistle

emptied into the yard
from culvert to fence

one loop
           or lap
then flung back

to where creek
swallows light

swallows the air
of any thing in flight

an effigy en route
swallows

           cicada   swift
storm   pizzicato
           red
                   sometimes
     red

one toad or two
swelling in the mulchlight

sweetgum & grass-lash

tracks of a three-
toed thing

chickweed & violet
the crickets flash
                          silent

clover & dandelion
the oak's roots soggen

hollow pine   slurped
with bores

the pollen staggers
& pools & clogs

leaves gather & clog

who built this bridge
& laid it across the line

I did   it's a silver bridge
                          sometimes

Notes

"Epithalamium" is for Sandrine Garet and Andrew Zawacki.

"Reign of Blisters" owes its title to Peter Rose.

"A Fine Piece of Equipment, Indeed" owes its title to Owl in the "Little Bear" animated series.

"With Something Like Determination, With Purpose" was written in Athens, Georgia in October 2002, shortly after the death of Kenneth Koch and while northern Virginia and the Washington, D.C. area were on full alert due to a series of sniper killings.

"Where We Stand Now" was written in Athens, Georgia and East Brunswick, New Jersey.

Addressed to Tomaž Šalamun, "Wings Without Birds" takes its opening move from James Schuyler's "A Stone Knife." The text in quotes is from Charles Darwin.

The title of "Where Hannibal Whomped the Romans" is from James Schuyler.

"What To Do With a Fat Rope of Old Vine" owes its title to Ann Lauterbach.

The title of "Life's Better on the Porch" is from a Starbuck's poster.

"Materniliad" quotes from Medbh McGuckian's "The Grief Machine" and borrows an image from the *Iliad* and the war in Iraq (2003–).

"Sometimes" is for Beckett. The poem builds on the work of Andrew Bird (specifically, his album *Noble Beast* and his entries in the "Measure for Measure" blog in the *New York Times*).